I0235823

IMAGES
*of America*

# SOUTH EUCLID

**CITY MAP.** This map shows the size and layout of the city of South Euclid, Ohio, an eastern suburb of Cleveland, Ohio. Over 22,000 people live within its 4.7 square miles. It borders on six other suburbs as well as a small section of the city of Cleveland itself. (South Euclid-Lyndhurst Historical Society.)

**ON THE COVER:** Special police officer Clifford Hoffman was an icon in South Euclid around the 1950s. He directed traffic and crossed pedestrians at the town's busiest intersection at Mayfield and Green Roads. His dynamic hand signals and loud, unaided whistles lent theater to this otherwise mundane task. (Sun Newspapers, now associated with the *Plain Dealer*.)

IMAGES
*of America*

# SOUTH EUCLID

South Euclid-Lyndhurst Historical Society

ARCADIA
PUBLISHING

Copyright © 2011 by South Euclid-Lyndhurst Historical Society
ISBN 9781531654917

Published by Arcadia Publishing
Charleston, South Carolina

Library of Congress Control Number: 2011940347

For all general information, please contact Arcadia Publishing:
Telephone 843-853-2070
Fax 843-853-0044
E-mail sales@arcadiapublishing.com
For customer service and orders:
Toll-Free 1-888-313-2665

Visit us on the Internet at www.arcadiapublishing.com

*This book is dedicated to the members of the South Euclid-Lyndhurst Historical Society and to all the people of South Euclid, past and present.*

# CONTENTS

# ACKNOWLEDGMENTS

The authors thank Thom Treer, author of *Lyndhurst*, for recommending our historical society for this project and Melissa Arnold, an author of *Cuyahoga Valley*, for encouraging us to take it on; the members of the Historical Society—especially curator Esther Eich, president Al Eich, and longtime members and South Euclid residents Ann Baird, Janet Dreyer, and Tony Palermo—for their support and help; Karen Zoller, director of the Notre Dame College Library, for much input and fact-checking; Mayor Georgine Welo, Michael Love, Keith Benjamin, and other South Euclid city staff for contacts and other help; our persistent but patient acquisitions editors at Arcadia, Melissa Basilone and Sandy Shalton, for helping us to keep on schedule; the many contributors to this book and our historical society; and our friends for putting up with our absences during this preparation.

Photographs were courtesy of the South Euclid-Lyndhurst Historical Society except as noted: (CPL) Cleveland Public Library Archives; (CPS) Carole Prochaska Smith family photographs; (JG) J. Goodman/The Image Project; (KZ) Karen Zoller; (McD) South Euclid McDonald's restaurant; (NASA) NASA website; (NDC) Notre Dame College Archives; (Speyer) Speyer family Warehouse Beverage photographs; (SUN) Sun Newspapers, now associated with the *Plain Dealer*; and (UH) Stanley A. Ferguson Archives, University Hospitals Case Medical Center.

The South Euclid-Lyndhurst Historical Society hopes you enjoy this publication.

—Bob McKimm and Frank Sillag

# INTRODUCTION

The glaciers of the last glacial period, known as the Wisconsin Glacial Episode, retreated 10,000 years ago, leaving the Great Lakes as reminders. Lake Erie is the southernmost of these. Native Americans often crossed the then swampy area that came to be known as Greater Cleveland, but there is no evidence of either a large or lengthy permanent settlement thereabouts. Thus, in 1796, when Gen. Moses Cleaveland of the Connecticut Militia arrived with a team of surveyors, these parts of Ohio were largely deserted.

Northern Ohio was the Western Reserve of the state of Connecticut, and while other states ceded their western reserves to the union, Connecticut was allowed to keep part of its holdings. The state sold much of this territory to the Connecticut Land Company, of which General Cleaveland was a director. The area's major city, Cleveland, was named after him. While the popular story is that the city lost the first *a* in the name when a newspaper headline in 1804 did not have room for it; earlier records exist with and without the first *a* in the name. Spelling was less restrictive at that time.

The surveyors found the going much tougher than they anticipated when they signed their two-year contracts, so they threatened to renege on them until General Cleaveland made them an offer they did not refuse: discounted land in a premium township. They also got naming rights and named it after their virtual patron saint, Euclid. Euclid was the Greek mathematician who developed plane geometry, which forms the basis for surveying. This township bordered Lake Erie where the shoreline runs pretty much northeast, giving this township about 40 percent more land and shoreline. None of the surveyors personally used these incentives; the land was sold to others.

Before long, four hamlets emerged in this township: Euclid, on the shoreline, and the more southerly South Euclid, Bluestone, and Euclidville. Bluestone was later absorbed by South Euclid. Since freight and passengers bound for Euclidville often ended up in the village of Euclid eight miles north, and vice versa, Euclidville held a contest for a new name and became Lyndhurst in 1921.

South Euclid sits mostly on a ridge known locally as "the Heights." These are the first western foothills hereabouts of the Allegheny Mountains. The city spans three waterways—Euclid Creek, Nine Mile Creek, and part of the Dugway Brook Watershed. Nine Mile Creek is largely covered now by Belvoir Boulevard. Euclid Creek eroded a deep, winding channel through layers of shale and dense, fine-grained sandstone. This created a scenic canyon and exposed the valuable rock named Euclid bluestone. Several quarries operated here and nearby. Their sites later became parks. Much of Euclid Creek lies within Euclid Creek Reservation, one of the Cleveland Metroparks that is a gem of the "Emerald Necklace" of parks draped around Cuyahoga County. The Civilian Conservation Corps (CCC) built many of the permanent structures in this park during the Great Depression.

Mayfield Road (US Route 322) is the major east-west road in town. It started as a dirt road, but in 1878, it became a wood plank toll road. Most industry grew up about this thoroughfare, and this is still true today. The city is largely sandwiched between inner-ring municipality Cleveland

Heights and the more suburban Lyndhurst. South Euclid began primarily as a farming community with grapes and strawberries as the principal crops cultivated. Basket factories sprang up to create containers for selling these products.

As Greater Cleveland's population grew, housing developments pushed out farms. Schools and churches abounded, as well as retail outlets and light industry. South Euclid then gained a reputation as a good place to raise a family. Many of these residents have matured and stayed, giving the city a diverse population.

# One

# THE EARLY YEARS

Euclid Township was settled shortly after the city of Cleveland itself and incorporated in 1809, a mere six years after Ohio became a state. Much of the land was cleared of both the huge trees present and the rattlesnakes that inhabited the ravines. Settlers largely moved in following the War of 1812 and established farms. Grapes and strawberries were popular crops and fostered the creation of small basket factories for the transport and sale of these crops. Local trees were mostly cooked to charcoal and toted to Cleveland.

Travel was largely on old Indian trails. South Euclid became defined by a mostly east-west trail then named State Road and now Mayfield Road (also known as US Route 322). The intersecting north-south road ran along the western ridge of Euclid Creek. It was called the Township Road to Warrensville, later Ruple Road, still later South Euclid Road, and finally, Green Road. This formed the major town center of South Euclid.

The Civil War sent several local citizens off to the fray but only one, Frank Prasse, did not return. He died in the Battle of Chancellorsville. When Harvey Hussong returned, he built the first frame house in the city, a style of construction he learned in his travels. It occupied a spot a little north of the northeast corner of Mayfield and Green Roads. Just south of there, the Old Stone School was built, educating children all the way through eighth grade.

Torrential rains often made roads impassable, especially for heavy-laden wagons, and so, in 1877, Mayfield Road was paved with wood planks for a distance of eight miles from Euclid Avenue to Gates Mills Hill and a toll charged for its use.

In the mid-1860s, the dense sandstone known as Euclid bluestone was discovered here in abundance. It launched an industry that survived for 40 years, terminated only when an improved mix for concrete became a cheaper acceptable material for sidewalks.

**THRESHING DAY.** This image was captured during harvest time at the Prasse farm in 1896. The farm was located near the intersection of Mayfield Road and Belvoir Boulevard. Nine Mile Creek largely runs (now in underground culverts) down the center of Belvoir Boulevard, so this farm enjoyed a ready supply of water. The steam engine at left back turns the belt to power the thresher.

**FRANK PRASSE.** Both Frank Prasse and his brother Frederick served in the Civil War, but only Frederick came back alive. Frank was killed in the Battle of Chancellorsville. He was the only South Euclid citizen to die in that war; however, the city was mostly farmland and sparsely populated at that time.

**PRASSE BASKET FACTORY.** The family built and operated a basket factory at Prasse and Green Roads, supplying containers for local farms and others. It was twice destroyed by fire but rebuilt. It finally ceased operation in 1966. This picture was taken around 1910.

Prasse Basket Factory
N. Side of Mayfield just
East of Francis Ct.     1910

**PRASSE EMPLOYEES.** The employees of the Prasse factory display basket bottoms as works in progress. The wood slats used had to be steamed to make them pliable. This purportedly was a very odiferous process, so the whole neighborhood knew when production was high.

**REKER BASKET FACTORY.** A rival factory began across Mayfield. This June 1903 photograph also shows stacks of the final product. The employees are listed as (first row) Carl Reker, Christ Hepker, Marg Meyers, and Daisy Mansfield; (second row) Ernst Fark, D. Reker, ? Kerpinsky, Walter Schafer, Joe Weigand, Frank Meyers, Charles Gardelo, Ed Hepker, and Fred Zilz.

BASKET SHIPPING. These baskets are on their way to market. The Prasse factory supplied baskets to farmers throughout northern Ohio. Some of the original baskets are displayed in the South Euclid-Lyndhurst Historical Museum.

**MAYFIELD TOLL ROAD.** From 1820, retired farmer Gordon Abbey tended the East Gate of the Mayfield Wood Plank Road (at Brainard Road) for about 20 years. This route was an attractive alternative to muddier east-west trails. The Lyndhurst gatehouse shown still stands but was relocated onto Brainard Road.

Toll Road Tolls

Two horse rig 2¢ per mile

One horse rig 1½¢

Man on horseback 1¢

Each head of stock with a Drover ½¢

**TOLL PRICES.** While this seems like a bargain today, these prices were in effect when the expression "another day, another dollar" really did describe a typical daily wage.

14

**DUNCAN McFARLAND.**
Shortly after the discovery of
bluestone, Duncan McFarland
bought a farm nearby and
established a quarry in 1867.
A total of four quarries
were in operation in South
Euclid by the mid-1880s.

DUNCAN McFARLAND

**BLUESTONE QUARRIES.** The
men working a little left
of center in this picture
give some notion of the
massive size of this quarry.

QUARRYING. The topsoil and shale had to be removed from above the sandstone and carted away, often by wheelbarrow. The rock slabs were separated by drilling down through the rock, filling the holes with dynamite, and setting it off, thus creating a crack between the slabs. Alternatively, workers filled the holes in winter with water, which froze, or in summer with wet saplings, which expanded; these would crack the rock. Drilled holes are visible on the leading edge of the slab in the center of this photograph.

**QUARRY POWER.** Steam engines supplied much of the power to move the huge blocks of stone. A steam whistle signaled the beginning and end of shifts, as well as other events. A long blast, signaling an accident, sent all the locals running to lend aid. Each quarry's whistle had a different tone so people could tell them apart.

**QUARRY MANPOWER.** Not much work could be done by machine. The quarries employed many workers, chiefly immigrants from Europe. They brought their language and religion. A Swedish church was built near Green and Anderson Roads, and a Swedish bakery was in operation on Green Road.

QUARRY MILL. The rock slabs then had to be sawed into the desired shapes and sizes. Railroad spurs were built to get the finished product down to Cleveland for shipment to its eventual destination. The railroad cars sometimes had to be pulled by horses, but fortunately, the trip was almost entirely downhill.

**BLUESTONE SIDEWALK.** In this picture, taken around 1990, Ethel Albaugh, a granddaughter of Duncan McFarland, is standing on a bluestone sidewalk. While truly gray, bluestone has a decided bluish tint when freshly cut, hence its name.

**QUARRYMEN.** The quarry workers were strong, rough men who worked hard and played hard. A small, local community sprang up, itself named Bluestone after the quarries. It sported two saloons and, alternatively, a Temperance Hall.

**CHARLES F. BRUSH.** Charles Brush was born in 1849 and raised on his parent's farm in Euclid Township. His advanced design of a dynamo (electric generator) had superior performance and lower maintenance than other designs.

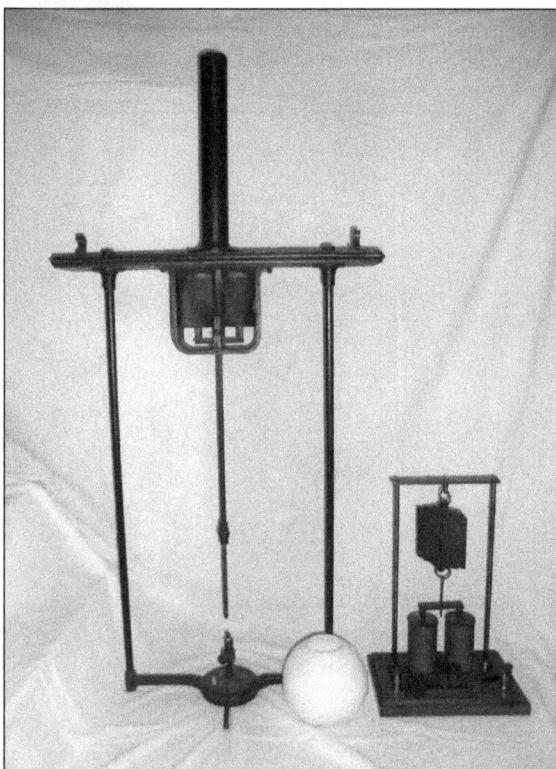

**ARC LAMP AND TEST EQUIPMENT.** Brush refined the design of the arc lamp and lit streets in Cleveland as well as many other major cities. In 1889, his firm was bought out by a company that merged into the General Electric Company. The South Euclid-Lyndhurst High School was named in honor of Brush. An arc lamp is on the left of the photograph. The apparatus on the right measures magnetic strength by its pull on a scale. Both devices now reside in the South Euclid-Lyndhurst Historical Museum.

# Two

# Into the 20th Century

Getting to and from South Euclid on foot or horseback was too limiting, so in 1898, an interurban railroad started running up and down Mayfield Road. It continued in operation until 1926. The county bought out the toll road stockholders, made the stretch a public highway, and paved it.

The Old Stone School was too small and too limited for use, so it was torn down in 1911. It was replaced by the larger Green Road School, offering classes all the way through 10th grade. In 1924, the South Euclid School System merged with the Lyndhurst School System.

Wealthy businessman William Telling built a mansion on his family's farm, but that is a chapter in itself (see chapter three). The Cuyahoga County Public Library, which now owns this estate and operates it as its South Euclid-Lyndhurst Branch, offers occasional tours of the mansion. The caretaker's cottage of this estate houses the South Euclid-Lyndhurst Historical Society.

The stock market crash of 1929 brought the Great Depression, with many people out of work in the 1930s. The Civilian Conservation Corps (CCC), part of Pres. Franklin D. Roosevelt's New Deal, employed thousands to work on projects around the nation. One camp was nearby and built trails and structures within Euclid Creek Park.

The end of World War II prompted tremendous growth in South Euclid. The city doubled in population in the four years, from 1946 to 1950.

**BLACKSMITH.** An early South Euclid industry was the blacksmith's shop, pictured here in 1897, on property owned by Lawrence Kirchner.

**TRUMPP'S HOTEL.** The only hotel ever built in South Euclid was the Trumpp's Hotel and Livery Stable on Mayfield by Sheffield Road, shown here in 1897.

**HOMECOMING AT HUSSONGS.** This 1911 picture shows, from left to right, (first row) William Quilliams, Dr. Burton, ? Gebauer, unidentified, Elizabeth Spencer, Adria Hussong (holding Harvey), and Margaret McFarland; (second row) James Harvey Hussong, ? Burton, William Telling, Mary Ann Ruple, Mrs. William Telling, and ? Quilliams.

**THE RED CARS.** The Cleveland & Eastern Railroad started transporting passengers up and down Mayfield Road in 1898. The electric-powered cars were painted red.

**FREIGHT CARS.** The railroad also hauled freight for farmers and merchants on this line.

**ALL ABOARD.** Schools asked the railway to quiet its whistle to stop distracting students, and cities asked them to limit the train's speed to only 15 miles per hour. The railway ceased operation in 1926.

CLEVELAND EASTERN RAILWAY FREIGHT CAR #55 AT GATES MILLS

**MAYFIELD AND GREEN ROADS, AROUND 1920.** This is the northeast corner of the intersection. Green Road School is in the background. Leo Larson is standing just in front of the Mayfield Road railroad tracks.

N. E. Corner Green & Mayfield Roads, Circa 1900. Green Road School, Leo Larson Standing Native Interurban Cartracks

**CAIN's REO BUS.** Independent bus lines served the eastern suburbs. The Cain Brothers Bus Company's REO bus was a highly regarded transport. It was built by the REO Motor Car Company, established by Ransom E. Olds, better known as the founder of the Olds Motor Company, which he left in a dispute. Olds Motor Company later became General Motors' Oldsmobile division.

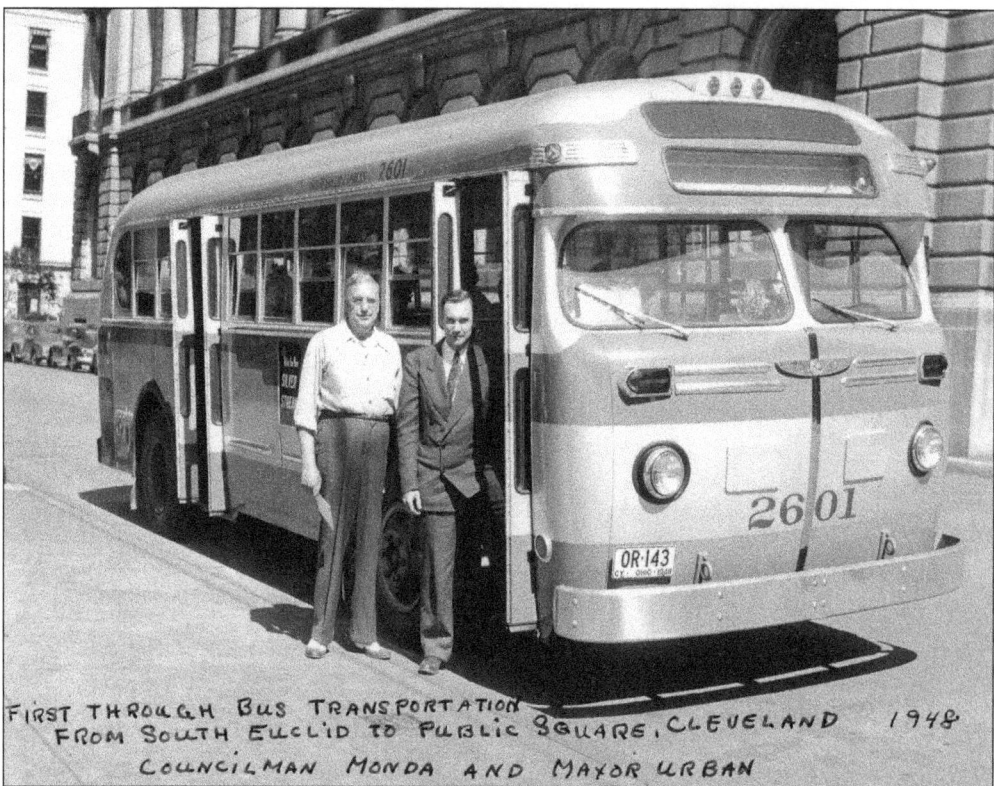

FIRST THROUGH BUS TRANSPORTATION FROM SOUTH EUCLID TO PUBLIC SQUARE, CLEVELAND 1948 COUNCILMAN MONDA AND MAYOR URBAN

**THE BUS DOWNTOWN.** South Euclid established a small bus line in 1948 to transport residents through Cleveland Heights and Cleveland's east side to Public Square. Riders could then transfer to Cleveland Transit System (CTS) buses to reach other parts of Cleveland. It was bought out by CTS. Later, CTS and other bus lines eventually merged into the Regional Transit Authority (RTA).

26

**MAYFIELD CENTRAL PARKING.** After the railroad ceased operation in 1926, the tracks were paved over and the center of the street became diagonal parking. In 1969, all parking on Mayfield Road was banned, which angered many of the merchants but dramatically reduced traffic accidents.

**CCC Camp.** Company 595 of the Civilian Conservation Corps, stationed near South Euclid, created many of the facilities now present in Cuyahoga County's Metropolitan Park Euclid Creek Reservation, within South Euclid.

**CCC at Work.** Around 1935, the CCC moved an elm tree to a better location. Unfortunately, they did not recognize how quickly Dutch Elm disease, which had invaded American shores a few years earlier, would spread.

**EUCLID CREEK FOOTPATH.** This is a 1935 photograph of a footpath dug out of the side of a cliff in the Euclid Creek Reservation. The major trail in the park is a two-mile path bordering the roadway. It follows the creek in a consistent and sometimes steep descent from Anderson to Highland Roads. Since this means a two-mile ascent the other direction, it is not a very popular path for bicyclists. (CPL.)

**EUCLID CREEK RECREATION.** This is one of several parking and recreational areas in the park. (CPL.)

**EUCLID CREEK PARK DEDICATION.** Preparations for the 1936 Euclid Creek Park dedication ceremony are shown in this image. (CPL.)

**EUCLID QUARRY ENTRANCE.** This 1941 photograph shows the entrance down the hill to the Quarry Picnic Area. (CPL.)

# *Three*

# WILLIAM TELLING AND HIS MANSION

William Telling and his wife, Mary Wespeaker Telling, settled in a log cabin on 23 acres of land in 1895. The hilly plot on the north side of Mayfield Road straddled a branch of Euclid Creek. A yellow farmhouse eventually replaced the cabin, and large barns were built. The Telling Mansion stands on part of that farm at 4645 Mayfield Road.

Mary Telling gave birth to 10 children, although not all survived. William Edward Telling Jr. was born on October 30, 1869. Young William's educational history is unclear; however, he and his siblings were certainly required to perform all of the chores on a 19th-century family farm. It is known that at an early age, he was selling strawberries and milk from the farm. At the age of 17, Will (as William Jr. was known) found his first job, operating a derrick in Bill Rolfe's bluestone quarry for $1.50 a day. Within two years, he had moved on to the position of conductor of a horse-drawn streetcar on Cleveland's Euclid Avenue. In the course of three and a half years on that job, Will Telling received a basic business education from the men who rode the streetcar.

Armed with $1,100 in savings, William Telling, age 23, purchased a Cleveland milk delivery route. In two years, he tired of driving a milk wagon and sold the route. Inspired by customer requests for ice cream, William teamed with his brother Charles and opened a restaurant and ice cream store on Euclid Avenue across from the elegant Lake View Cemetery. The brothers made small batches of ice cream in the basement. The business flourished, and on December 12, 1895, the Telling Brothers Company was incorporated. With William E. Telling Jr. as president, the company increased sales of ice cream and other dairy products while moving to larger facilities as capital became available. For years, the Telling Brothers Company and the Bell Vernon Dairy Farms Company had shared space and facilities in a building on Willson Avenue. They merged in 1915 as the Telling-Belle Vernon Company.

William E. Telling Jr. began building a mansion on the southern six acres of the family farm in 1928. The 26-room mansion and two outbuildings were completed in 1931 at a cost of $700,000. Telling lived in the mansion until his death in 1938. It changed hands several times and has been the South Euclid-Lyndhurst Branch of the Cuyahoga County Public Library System since 1951.

**THE MAN.** This autographed photograph of William Edward Telling Jr. is probably from the late 1920s. The framed original is displayed in the museum of the South Euclid-Lyndhurst Historical Society.

**TELLING FARMHOUSE AND FAMILY.** Shown below in about 1900 is the family farmhouse on Mayfield Road. In front, from left to right, are children Charles, Emma, Eva, John, William Jr., Frank, father William Telling Sr., mother Mary Wespeaker Telling, and Walter.

**TELLING MILK WAGON.** A one-horsepower Telling milk delivery wagon shares an unidentified brick street with an automobile.

**MILK BOTTLES.** Of the Telling Belle Vernon bottles displayed, the two with bulbous necks are the most significant. In the days before commercially supplied milk was homogenized, gravity separated cream and skim milk in the bottle. Telling's innovative "Cream Top" bottle captured the lighter cream in the neck of the bottle where it could be removed with a special spoon.

**THE ICE CREAM STORE.** A Telling delivery wagon stands in front of the Telling Brothers ice cream shop. A man beyond the horse stands on a stone block provided to aid in mounting a horse or entering a carriage.

**MAKING ICE CREAM.** A man (possibly one of the Telling brothers) pours cream into a 3.5-gallon hand-cranked ice cream freezer in the basement of the shop. To the right is a bin of crushed ice.

**TELLING ICE CREAM WAS POPULAR.** The Telling Brothers ice cream business was very successful and grew into a larger facility. Several employees are shown by a line of ice cream freezers. The freezers were cranked by a line shaft above, which was driven by a gasoline engine (not shown).

**CATERING BUSINESS.** William Telling was involved in many business ventures. Here, the kitchen staff of his catering business pauses for this photograph.

THE MANSION. In 1928, architect John Sherwood Kelly began designing a 26-room mansion for William E. Telling Jr. It was built by Keys-Treuhaft Construction Company on the site of

the Telling family farm at 4645 Mayfield Road in South Euclid. William Telling and some close relatives moved into this $700,000 home in 1931.

HOUSE OF MANY STYLES. The rear (north) view of the mansion shows the stone on the lower story, decorative brick above, and timber and stucco gables. Custom-made roof tiles, chimney pots, and finials cap it off.

LIFE AS A LIBRARY. The Cuyahoga County Public Library System acquired the mansion and the southern portion of the Telling family farm in 1951. The fully glazed conservatory and aviary were enclosed in brick walls and tile roofs. This present view shows the former conservatory to the left and the octagonal aviary near right.

**RELAXING READING ROOM.** The south end of the conservatory is still graced by the original fountain and many plants. It serves as an art display area and reading room in the library. This shows in part why Nancy Pearl, author of *Book Lust*, chose this library for her *USA Today* list of "10 great places to find a nook and read a book."

**GRAND ENTRY.** The elegant foyer displays the rich detailing of the interior. A grand wrought-iron chandelier hangs from an ornate plaster ceiling above a patterned marble floor. Gothic stone archways and deeply carved doors set the tone for the rest of the house.

**GATEHOUSE.** The mansion grounds include two outbuildings. The gatehouse, directly fronting Mayfield Road, is shown with the main gate in the foreground. Note the rich detailing of the masonry and the wrought-iron fence, gates, and lanterns. Telling moved into this first-erected building while the rest of the mansion was finished. It later served as his secretary's quarters.

**NOW A MUSEUM.** The caretaker/gardener's cottage is now occupied by the South Euclid-Lyndhurst Historical Museum. The building is connected to the mansion by a covered driveway (in the shadow to the right) and tunnels belowground. The deep basement housed the coal bin, boilers, and other mechanical equipment.

**North Detail.** This partial view of the north side shows the heavy stone exterior of the partially exposed basement. Above that is the ornate brick and stone cladding of the first and second floors.

**Pre-Restoration.** The Cuyahoga County Public Library System undertook a sensitive restoration of the landmark building. The concrete block structure to the far left was removed, and the area was converted to an entrance to the library basement. The bricked-up archway in the extreme lower right was originally the entry to the 10-car garage in the basement.

**FOUNTAIN ON THE PORCH.** An elegant tile fountain and wrought-iron light fixtures still grace what was originally a semi-enclosed porch.

**ORNAMENTAL INTERIOR.** This Gothic arch door is decorated with deep carvings and elegant hardware. The original architectural drawings went so far as to detail the carvings on the doors.

# Four

# CHURCHES, SCHOOLS, AND
# A HOSPITAL

The Methodist church was originally built at Mayfield and Green Roads, but it later moved a little south on Green Road. The immigrant quarrymen brought their religion with them and built a Swedish church near Green and Anderson Roads. Other religions and their houses of worship abounded.

In 1917, the locale now known as Lyndhurst learned that Euclid Township was about to close Richmond Road School. Their students would then have to go to South Euclid or to Claribel (now named Richmond Heights). By incorporating, citizens could control their own system and the unincorporated systems around them. The people incorporated as the village of Euclidville in mid-1917. Later, in 1917, South Euclid also incorporated as a village, presumably so Lyndhurst, in turn, would not control its schools. In 1923, these two villages faced a growing problem—Lyndhurst had no high school, and South Euclid's was too small. Dr. J.E. Rowland of South Euclid supported merging the two systems. He was a member of the county board of education, which had the authority to do this. Over the objections of many from both villages, as well as an unsuccessful legal challenge, it happened. In late 1926, a new high school was built on what had been the Henry Melcher farm and part of the Dodsworth farm, just east of South Euclid in the western edge of Lyndhurst.

In 1928, Notre Dame College, a Catholic women's college, opened its doors on Green Road near Cedar Road. In 2001, it became coed. Regina High School, an all-girls school, was established adjacent to it in 1953 and operated until lack of enrollment forced it to close in 2010.

The Order of the King's Daughters was a fraternal organization comprised of local circles organized to perform charitable functions. The Cleveland group was named Rainbow Circle and started with nine of the daughters of Cleveland's wealthiest families on Thanksgiving Day in 1887. They first had a center at 105th Street and Lakeshore Boulevard to treat children, primarily those with rickets, polio, diphtheria, scarlet fever, and other crippling diseases. In 1901, the group relocated to a Lyndhurst location, but it burned down on Halloween in 1904. They then moved to rental facilities in South Euclid, eventually building the 125-bed Rainbow Hospital at Green and Rainbow Roads in 1928. These childhood diseases became increasingly avoidable and treatable, causing the Rainbow Hospital's 1971 merger with University Hospital's Babies and Children's Hospital on Cleveland's east side.

First Church built in South
Euclid by the Methodists in
1883. nr. NW corner of Green
MOVED TO 1534 SOUTH GREEN Rd. 1898

**METHODIST CHURCH.** Built in 1883, this church was moved 15 years later from the northwest corner of Mayfield and Green Roads closer to its current location.

MENTHODIST CHURCH OF SOUTH EUCLID DEDICATED 1914
ON SOUTH GREEN ROAD        RAZED    1966

**METHODIST CHURCH II.** Built in 1914 and expanded in 1924, it continued in use even after 1957, when a more modern building was erected alongside. It was razed in 1966.

SOUTH EUCLID
United Methodist Church

**METHODIST CHURCH III.** This 1957 building continues in use as the South Euclid–Hillcrest United Methodist Church. It currently provides space for a summertime farmers' market and many other community activities.

45

Swedish Lutheran Church in
Metro Park, Razed 1930.

**SWEDISH LUTHERAN CHURCH.** This small building was constructed near Green and Anderson Roads. It primarily served quarrymen and their families. It was razed around 1930.

**ST. JOHN LUTHERAN CHURCH.**
German was the original language
of choice of this congregation,
but services changed to English
around the 1920s. This is how
the church appeared in 1966.

**ST. JOHN LUTHERAN CHURCH
AND PARSONAGE.** In 1854, the
German settlers purchased the
land where this church, school,
and cemetery still stand. The
parsonage gave way to a small
strip of retail stores well after this
1910 photograph was taken.

**CHURCH OF THE MASTER.** This Baptist church left Ninety-seventh Street and Euclid Avenue in Cleveland to build this 1952 structure at Quarry Drive and Monticello Boulevard.

**ST. MARGARET MARY.** This Catholic church, built during 1949 and 1950, was located in the then nearly vacant hamlet of Bluestone where Bluestone Road meets Belvoir Boulevard.

**ST. GREGORY THE GREAT.** In 1922, this church was built on property that had been owned by former mayor E.J. Foote.

**NEWER ST. GREGORY.** In 1961, the church erected this newer, larger building. In 2010, St. Greg's merged with St. Margaret Mary to form Sacred Heart of Jesus Parish.

OLD STONE SCHOOL. While classes had been held in various locations, this school, built in 1865, centralized them. Classes through the eighth grade were held here. This photograph was taken in 1907.

*Our beloved Teacher- Miss Lotti Kerckoff lilac time - notice boquets on boys and girls*

**Old Stone School House ~ Primary Grades South Euclid ~ 1898**

OLD STONE SCHOOL, 1898 CLASS. These are the 1898 primary grades students at Old Stone School. This picture was taken during lilac time in the spring, and the teacher, Lotti(?) Kerckoff, provided bouquets for both the boys and girls.

**Old Stone School Grammar, Fifth through Eighth Grades.** This c. 1910 image depicts some of the last students at this school. It was torn down in 1911. Pictured are, from left to right, (first row) Walter Dorsch with dog Dewey, Arden Rowland, unknown, Ethel Mae Morlock, Ruth Cliff, Helen Brandis, Esther Sherwitz, Irma Brandis, and William Dorsch; (second row) ? Miller, Homer Rowland, Ed Markowitz, unknown, Maurice Bilkey, Henry Faust, Lyle McFarland, unknown, Earl Gerstenberger, Theresa Markowitz, Leo Murray, Francis Telling, and Henry Office; (third row) ? Johnson, Alice Worthington, Grace Jordan, Esther Miller, Mable Dorsch, unknown, Elvey Albright, and teacher ? Lash.

**GREEN ROAD SCHOOL.** Old Stone School was torn down in 1911, and Green Road School was built on that site in 1912. It offered classes all the way through the 10th grade.

**GREEN ROAD SCHOOLCHILDREN.** This is a class in the first year at the newly built school.

GREEN ROAD SCHOOL, THIRD AND FOURTH GRADES IN 1915. Pictured are, from left to right, (first row) Leonard Anderson, Lee Hamilton, Roy Brott, George Urban, Thomas Beaver, Clarence Larson, William Freeman, and L. Zack; (second row) Ellen Sersinger, Ruby Crane, unknown, Laurel Krieg, Mary Wilkins, Margaret Luster, Irma Renner, and Anna Vanisky; (third row) Frank Zeller, Carl Anderson, Henry Telling, Kenneth Telling, teacher Bessie Wells, Harvey Hussong, John Ruskai, and Albert Beaver.

RICHMOND ROAD SCHOOL
S.W. CORNER MAYFIELD Rd.

IRCA 1920

**RICHMOND ROAD SCHOOL.** Sitting just east of South Euclid in Lyndhurst, this school is now the offices of the South Euclid-Lyndhurst Board of Education. The Euclid Township's threatened closing of this school resulted in both Lyndhurst and South Euclid incorporating as villages in 1917 so they could control their own school systems.

1941 photo of the
Victory Park School.

Photo by James J. Kelley,
staff photographer of the
South Euclid Citizen.

**VICTORY PARK SCHOOL.** Victory Park on Victory Drive, just west of Green Road, had a memorial commemorating World War I. An elementary school was built there in 1921. This photograph was taken in 1941. (SUN.)

**SCHOOL IN WINTER.** Here is a closer view of the entrance. In 1980, the school was closed due to low attendance in the post–baby boom years. In 1983, the Mayfield frontage was sold to Acme, a food store chain, which built a store as well as the city's community center at the site. The food store is now part of the Giant Eagle chain.

**DR. JUSTIN E. ROWLAND.** Dr. Rowland came to South Euclid in 1891, and after completing his medical education at Cleveland Medical College (which became part of Case Western Reserve University), he practiced homeopathic medicine at Huron Road Hospital. He became a member of the Euclid Township School Board and, later, the Cuyahoga County School Board, where he helped engineer the merger of the South Euclid and Lyndhurst school systems. He also helped found the South Euclid Savings and Loan (now part of KeyBank) and was an active member of Kiwanis, the Citizen's League, and the Methodist Church. He married Adah Mighton, who was also a physician.

BRUSH HIGH SCHOOL 1928

**BRUSH HIGH SCHOOL.** Completed at a cost of $468,151, Brush High School began classes in January 1926 with 412 students in grades 7 through 12. It sported 16 classrooms plus an auditorium, a library, and a cafeteria.

BRUSH HIGH
BUILT 1927

**BRUSH AT NIGHT.** As might be expected, this school, named after the renowned arc-lamp inventor, is well lit. Its athletic field was allegedly the first test site for the General Electric Company's quartz halogen lighting for this purpose.

58

**BRUSH AERIAL VIEW.** Looking roughly northwest, Mayfield Road is in the lower left of this image. Brush High School's circular drive is in the center.

1967
DR. MARVIN MAIRE SUPT. SCHO

**SCHOOL SUPERINTENDENT.** Dr. Marvin Maire was the South Euclid-Lyndhurst school superintendent from 1966 to 1972, during the post–World War II baby boom.

**BRUSH TEACHERS.** Three well-known teachers in 1966 are, from left to right, Michael "Mac" Palermo, John Welser, and Karl Keller. Palermo was also assistant coach under Welser and became head coach and later principal of Memorial Junior High. In addition to coaching, Welser taught industrial arts. Keller taught science and also developed the school library system. He later served as principal of the high school.

1966 BRUSH HIGH TEACHERS

"MAC" PALERMO          JOHN C. WELSER          KARL N. KELLER

BASKETBALL. In 1917, Green Road School organized its first basketball team.

BASEBALL. Baseball leagues also formed. Mark Negrelli, a city councilman and founder of Glenridge Machine Company, is on the right; the baseball field was dedicated to him. (SUN.)

Dedication of the new St. Gregory the Great Elementary School by the Most Rev. Archbishop Edward Hoban, April 21, 1950.

**ST. GREGORY THE GREAT SCHOOL.** Schooling at St. Gregory's began in 1925 with four portable classrooms borrowed from the nearby St. Ann Church. In April 1950, Archbishop Hoban dedicated the new 17-room school at St. Gregory's to Our Lady of Fatima. (SUN.)

**FIFTH GRADE.** This is St. Gregory's fifth-grade class during the 1946–1947 school year. (CPS.)

**ST. JOHN LUTHERAN SCHOOL.** Classes at St. John started in 1860. The original building unit was constructed in 1927, then moved and renovated in 1954. It was added to in 1966, about the time this photograph was taken.

**ST. JOHN SCHOOLCHILDREN.** This 1889 photograph of students and teacher includes, from left to right, (first row) Edward Prasse, Mary Bindbeutel, and Willy Nitske; (second row) Christ Obrock, Nora Farn, Martha Schaefer, Louise Prasse, teacher ? Hoffmeyer, Mathilda Faust, Minnie Melcher, Henrietta Prasse, and John Abil; (third row) Fred Elbrecht, Richard Lossner, William Wischmeyer, Fred Fark, and Henry Kuhlman.

South Euclid Lutheran School ~ 1889

**REGINA HIGH SCHOOL.** The Catholic Order of the Sisters of Notre Dame first came to the United States in 1874 from Coesfeld, Germany. The order moved its college to South Euclid in 1928 and added a high school just north of it in 1953. (NDC.)

**REGINA GROUNDS.** An all-girl Catholic high school, under the auspices of the Sisters of Notre Dame, began offering classes in the fall of 1953 with 148 girls and a faculty of 12 Sisters. (NDC.)

**REGINA DEDICATION.** Pictured is the procession to the 1954 dedication of Regina High School. (NDC.)

**DEDICATION.** Pictured is the dedication ceremony. Because of declining enrollment, Regina had to cease operations and graduated its last class in 2011. (NDC.)

REGINA HIGH SCHOOL
SOUTH GREEN RD., SOUTH EUCLID, OHIO
ARCHITECT: JOHN F. LIPAJ & ASSOCIATES
GENL. CONTRACTOR: R.P. CARBONE CONST. CO.
NO.___ DATE___ VIEW___

**REGINA ADDITION.** In 1962, Regina added 20 classrooms and an expanded library. (NDC.)

**DRAWING ROOM.** Seen here is a classroom in Regina High School during the 1950s. (NDC.)

**WEIGHT WATCHERS.** In this 1980s photograph, a couple of unidentified Regina High School students are observed while they use a scale to determine the mass of a laboratory sample. They are watched by Sr. Mary Catherine Caine, SND, who taught science from 1979 to 1984. (NDC.)

**REGINA LIBRARY.** The Regina High School Library is pictured here in the 1950s. (NDC.)

**NOTRE DAME COLLEGE SITE PREPARATION.** In 1926, a steam shovel dug the ground, but the dirt was carted away by less technologically advanced means. (NDC.)

**NOTRE DAME COLLEGE ADMINISTRATION BUILDING.** This is the completed building known then simply as "the College." It contained all of the facilities, including a dormitory. The next building, a separate dormitory named Hark's Hall, was not erected until 1955. (NDC.)

**Moving into Notre Dame.** In or around 1931, this group of students moves into Notre Dame College. Note the dress styles and luggage. (NDC.)

**Notre Dame Chapel.** Pictured is the chapel in the Administration Building of Notre Dame College in 1928. A Holtkamp pipe organ was installed in the choir loft in 1930. Located in Cleveland, Ohio, Holtkamp still builds organs. (NDC.)

**TENNIS, ANYONE?** Notre Dame College coeds take to the tennis courts in 1940. The courts were located near Division and Lawnway Roads. Note the dresses and the shoes. (NDC.)

**NDC LIBRARY.** This image of the Notre Dame College library was captured in 1928. A card catalog sits just to the right of the front desk. A separate library building, the Clara Fritzsche Library, opened in 1971. This space is now the Admissions Office. (NDC.)

**AIR-RAID WARDENS.** The Notre Dame College faculty trained in 1942 to use gas masks in the event of poisonous gas attacks on the United States during World War II. (NDC.)

**WAR BONDS.** Patriotic Notre Dame College students did their part in 1943 by selling war bonds and stamps. Marie Guarino (left), class of 1946, and Jean Boggins, class of 1945, are pictured here. (NDC.)

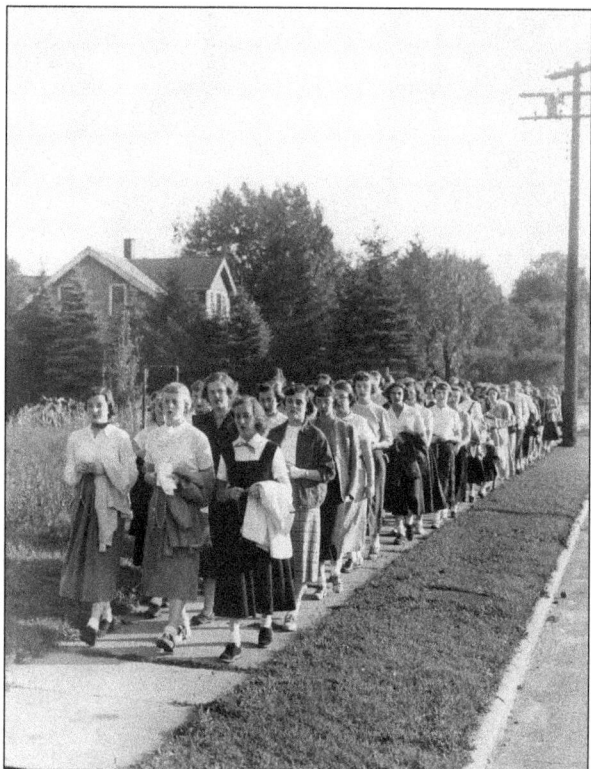

**PILGRIMAGE.** In 1950, the young women of Notre Dame College pray the rosary as they walk north on Green Road to Providence Heights (also known as Our Lady of Lourdes Shrine) nearly six miles away in Euclid, Ohio. (NDC.)

**MODERN DANCE.** Three Notre Dame College students perform modern dance in the gymnasium located below the Administration Building. This photograph was taken around 1950. (NDC.)

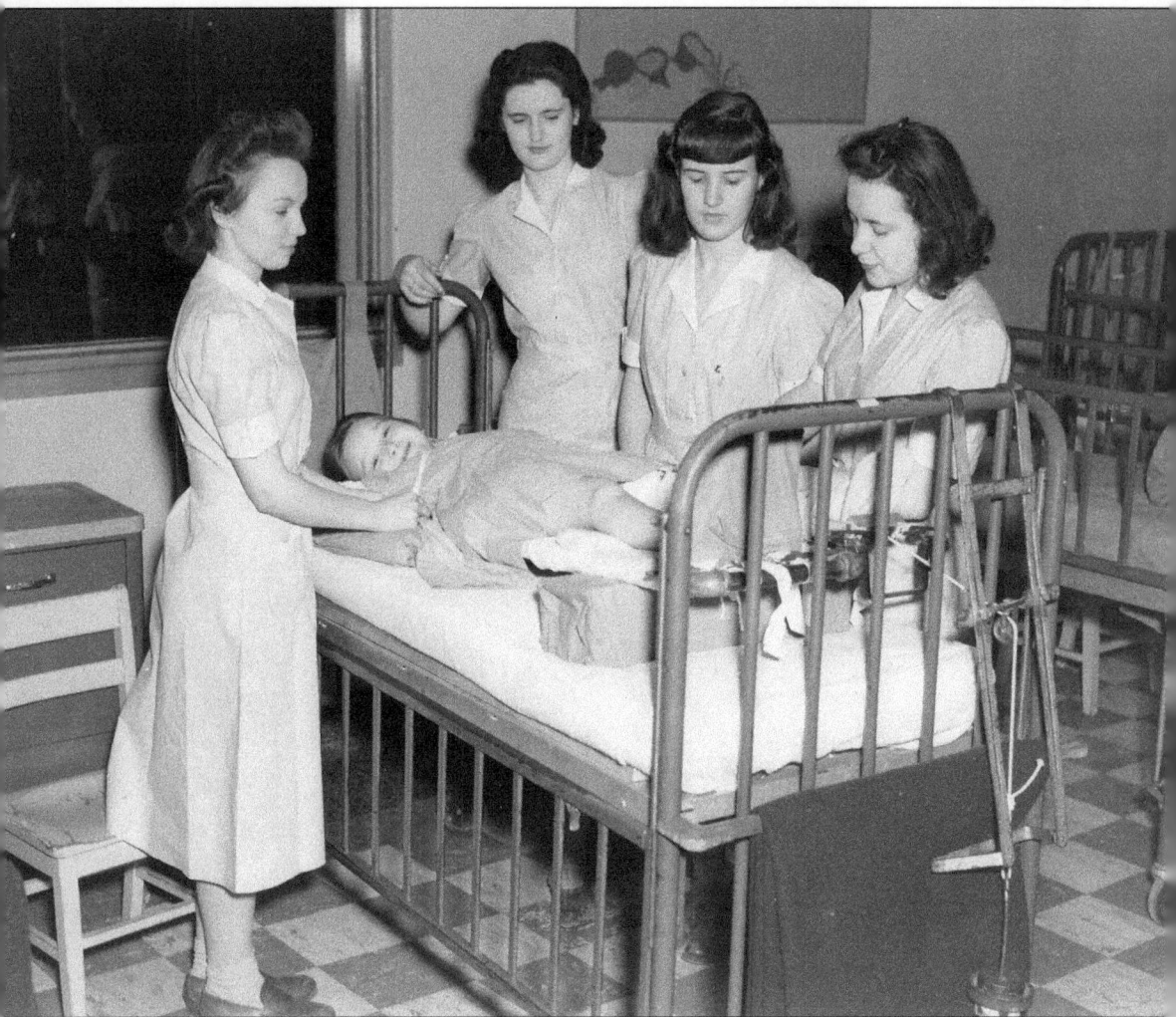

**NURSES AIDES.** For many years, Notre Dame College students worked or volunteered at nearby Rainbow Hospital for Crippled and Convalescent Children. Some even resided at the hospital, walking the short distance to campus. Here, in 1944, these students are working as nurses aides. (NDC.)

**RAINBOW HOSPITAL.** After years at locations in Cleveland, Lyndhurst, and rented facilities in South Euclid, Rainbow Hospital broke ground on a new 125-bed facility a bit north of where Notre Dame College was under construction. By 1971, so many of the childhood diseases (polio,

In the photograph, stamped markings read:

THE SELDEN EXCAVATING

THEW

10-28-27
№ 1-2

Rainbow Hospital
Franz C. Warner, W. H. McCormac
Architects,
The Craig-Curtiss Co.

diphtheria, and others) had cures or had been brought under control that two area children's hospitals were no longer needed, and Rainbow merged into University Hospitals Babies and Children's Hospital at its University Circle location in the city of Cleveland. (UH.)

HOSPITAL. The Rainbow Hospital buildings were shaped in an arc, not unlike its namesake. It continued in operation until 1971, when it merged with University Hospital's pediatric facility and relocated to Cleveland's University Circle, becoming Rainbow Babies and Children's Hospital. (UH.)

**FRESH AIR.** Three staples of the hospital's treatments were wholesome food, fresh air, and sunshine. Hospital staff allowed the patients out on the grounds whenever feasible. (UH.)

**RIN TIN TIN.** A very popular children's television show in the mid-1950s, *The Adventures of Rin Tin Tin* featured a German shepherd as its animal star. The patients at Rainbow Hospital were delighted when "Rinty" paid them a visit. He may have had some help tying that bib on—just like some of the children. (UH.)

# Five

# PEOPLE, PLACES, AND THINGS

S. Bruce Lockwood was publisher of the weekly newspaper the *South Euclid Citizen* from its founding in 1924 until his ill health necessitated its sale in 1946, covering a span of 1,168 consecutive weeks. The paper transferred several times in the next three years until it was consolidated with the *South Euclid Messenger*. This latter paper was bought by the Sun Newspaper chain in 1958 and continues today as the *Sun Messenger*.

Hussong House, originally built after the Civil War, was the first frame house in South Euclid. It was destroyed by fire in the late 1800s but promptly rebuilt at its site on the east side of Green Road, a little north of Mayfield. It was a popular gathering spot, as many photographs suggest. The South Euclid-Lyndhurst Historical Society has a program for recognizing century homes in those cities.

The Mayfield Road and Green Road intersection and the area nearby have reinvented themselves very frequently. While South Euclid has historically been mostly a bedroom community, it also supported many small businesses—most of them savory, one not so much.

S. BRUCE LOCKWOOD

**NEWSPAPERMAN.** S. Bruce Lockwood published the *South Euclid Citizen* from 1924 to 1946—a span of 22 years, or 1,168 consecutive weekly issues.

**FRANK SNELL.** Frank Snell was a much-beloved Boy Scout and youth leader.

1967
FRANK SNELL    BOY SCOUT LEADER    98

**PRASSE.** Frederick (1867–1942) and Pauline Prasse are pictured here. Frederick was also a founder of the South Euclid Savings and Loan.

**HUDSON'S GAS.** A gas station graced the northwest corner of Mayfield and Green Roads. It naturally offered full service. Green Road School is across the street, and the South Euclid Savings and Loan is to its right. In 1928, the South Euclid Savings and Loan was built so close to the school that the school changed its main entrance to Green Road.

**FREDDIE CARLONE ORCHESTRA.** During the big band era, Freddie Carlone put together an orchestra that played in many Cleveland ballrooms and toured as well. Freddie's brother Anthony Carlone, a South Euclid councilman, played in and managed the band. Freddie was president of the Cleveland musician's union and best man at Perry Como's wedding.

**PERRY COMO.** A Pennsylvania barber named Pierino "Perry" Como responded to an open mike invitation in Cleveland to sing with the Freddie Carlone Orchestra. The band offered him a job, and Perry toured with the group for three years, rehearsing in a Sheridan Road basement. He considered declining an offer with Chicago's Ted Weems Orchestra, but Freddie urged him to make this career move. This led "Mr. C." to recordings, radio, and a popular TV show in the 1950s and 1960s. This autographed photograph was sent to Mayor George Urban.

**WILLIAM T. ARNOS.** Arnos was a real estate developer noted for a three-story building at the southeast corner of Mayfield and Green Roads and for developing Belvoir Boulevard and the surrounding streets.

92 WILLIAM T. ARNOS

**ROYAL NEIGHBORS.** Royal Neighbors was a ladies fraternal nonprofit life insurance operation that also stressed volunteering in the community. Pictured here is the local group around 1940.

100 ROYAL NEIGHBORS LODGE CIRCA 19

**GARAGE.** In the early 1920s, the Thorsell Brothers business was located near the northwest corner of Mayfield and Green Roads.

**HUDSON'S GAS STATION.** This tiny gasoline station was situated at the northwest corner of Mayfield and Green Roads in 1938.

**HUSSONG HOUSE I.** James Harvey Hussong, standing on the porch stairs, returned from the Civil War and brought with him an idea for frame house construction.

**HUSSONG HOUSE II.** The original house was destroyed by fire in 1898, so J.H. rebuilt it. His home on the east side of Green Road, just north of the school, was a popular place for gatherings.

**Speyer's.** Adolph Speyer (left) opened his first store in South Euclid in April 1940. His father, Aaron Speyer (right), worked with him. (Speyer.)

**Deli.** Speyer's Creamery and Delicatessen was located at 4434 Mayfield Road, just east of Garden Road. (Speyer.)

**SPEYER'S BEVERAGE.** In the late 1940s, Adolph Speyer opened a beverage store on Garden Road behind Bemis Florist. He called it Warehouse Beverage, since the building looked like a warehouse. (Speyer.)

**WAREHOUSE BEVERAGE.** In 1951, the store moved to this location at 4364 Mayfield Road (at Sheffield Road). The family still operates this business today. (Speyer.)

**MAY GREEN PAINT AND WALLPAPER.** This Smith family business was located in the parking lot behind the bank. The family still owns much of the Maymore Shopping Center.

**THE SMITHS.** Members of the Smith family posing inside their store are, from left to right, Walter, Walter Sr., and Tim. (CPS.)

**BIEGER'S STORE.** Bieger's Store was located at the southwest corner of Mayfield and Green Roads, as shown in this 1918 photograph.

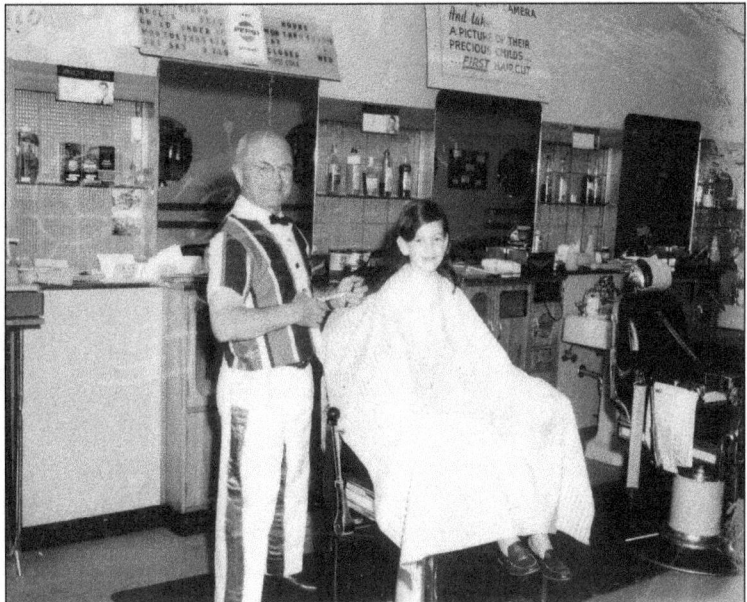

**ERNY'S BARBER SHOP.** Ernest Stoetzer's barbershop was built on part of the spot that John Ruple's House (see page 95) once occupied. In 1967, when this photograph was taken, an adult haircut cost $2.25, and a child's haircut was cheaper—except on weekends.

**BILKEY'S.** Bilkey's Confectionery Store was located on Mayfield Road east of Green Road around 1890.

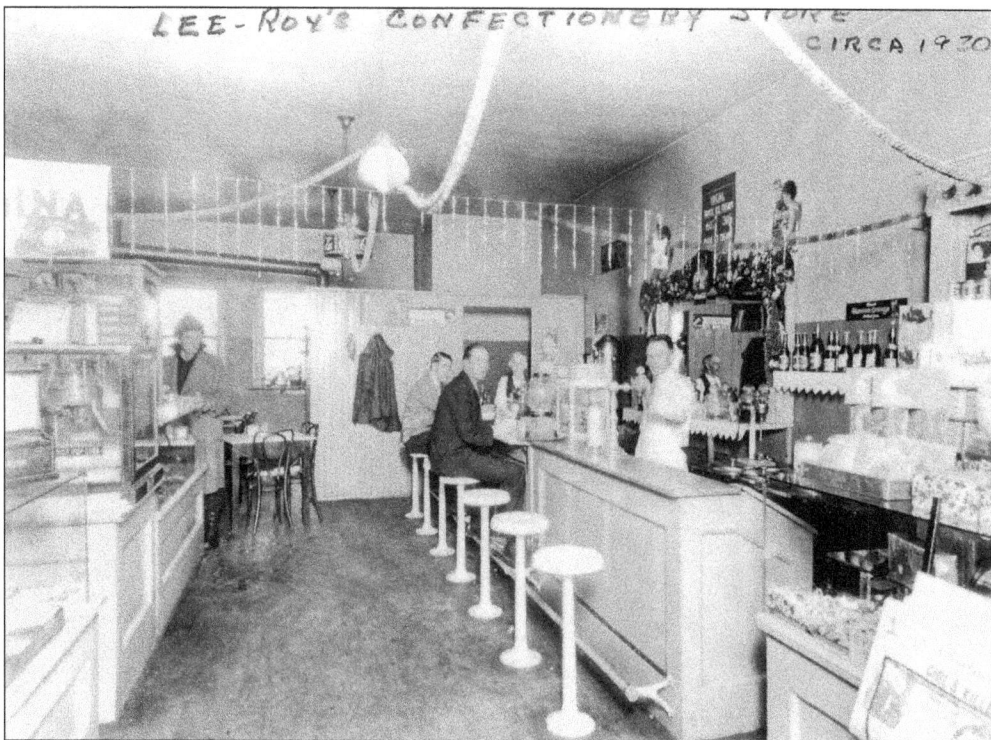

**LEE-ROY'S.** Lee-Roy's Confectionery Store is pictured here around 1930. Roy Hamilton stands behind the counter. The others in the photograph are unidentified.

RUPLE HOUSE. Deacon John Ruple was among South Euclid's earliest citizens. This is Ruple House in 1888.

McDONALD'S. Around 1963, a fast-food restaurant chain entered the Cleveland area, selling 15¢ hamburgers. The South Euclid location was among the first in the Cleveland area, and it was built on the property where Ruple House once stood. A couple renovations later, it still stands. McDonald's was noted for careful market research in site selection. (McD.)

**MAYFIELD EAST.** This photograph was taken facing east from McDonald's. Standard Oil of Ohio (SOHIO) became part of British Petroleum (BP) but kept its US headquarters in Cleveland until BP's acquisition of Chicago-based Amoco. (McD.)

**MAY-GREEN NORTHEAST.** Seen across the street from the then new McDonald's, Mancuso's was a popular food store. Just to the left of these buildings, Cleveland Trust became Ameritrust and was absorbed by Society, which became part of KeyBank. (McD.)

**Sandwiched.** Originally sandwiched between the General Store and Erny's Barber Shop, McDonald's later took over the General Store spot to use for parking. (McD.)

**Hangout.** Because of cheap prices and a parking lot, McDonald's became something of a teen hangout at one time. The city then passed an ordinance against eating in cars, which, if it still exists, is no longer enforced. (McD.)

First presentation of
Colors by South Euclid
Post 308, the American
Legion. Memorial Day, 19

AMERICAN LEGION. In 1931, thirteen World War I veterans, led by teacher Karl Keller, assembled to form American Legion Post No. 308. This is the first presentation of colors (flags) by that unit, on Memorial Day in 1932.

AMERICAN LEGION AUXILIARY. The American Legion Auxiliary was formed in 1931. This is the group's first formal initiation ceremony held on February 1, 1940.

FLOOD AT MAYFIELD-GREEN. All of South Euclid is more than 500 feet above sea level, including Lake Erie and its myriad feeder streams, some which run through South Euclid. A late-May 1959 storm overwhelmed the banks of these waterways, flooding the Mayfield and Green Roads intersection. (SUN.)

FLOOD AT BELVOIR. The Mayfield Road and Belvoir Boulevard intersection fared worse. The region has since begun an extensive project of storm interceptors and other waterway projects to make a recurrence of a flood unlikely.

GOLDEN JUBILEE. August 1967 was South Euclid's 50th anniversary as a village, which prompted an exceptionally large home-day celebration. Royal Castle in the background was noted for its sliders (2.5-inch hamburgers, sold by the dozen) and birch beer (similar to root beer).

PARADE CLOWNS. Costumed figures dotted the parade and passed out candy to the children lining the streets.

**50-Year Residents.** During South Euclid's Golden Jubilee, these folks are there to celebrate. South Euclid used to have a "home day" the first Sunday in August, but the cost of this became prohibitive, and it was recently discontinued.

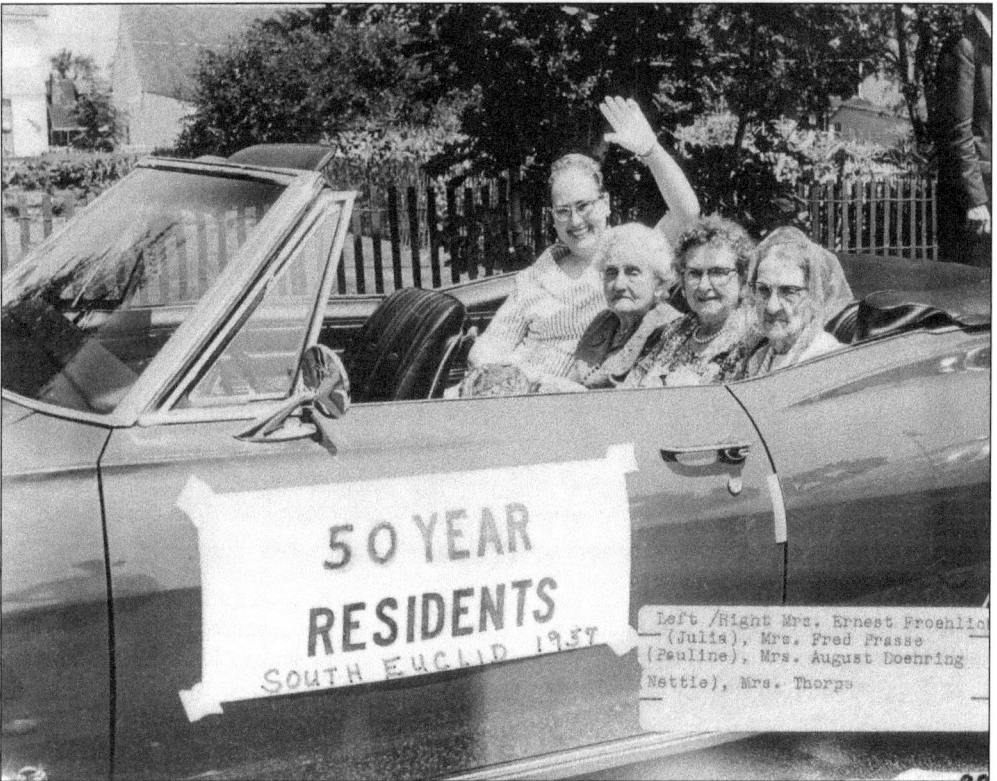

**Golden Residents.** Shown here are, from left to right, Julia Froehlich (Ernest), Pauline Prasse (Fred), Nettie Doehring (August), and ? Thorpe.

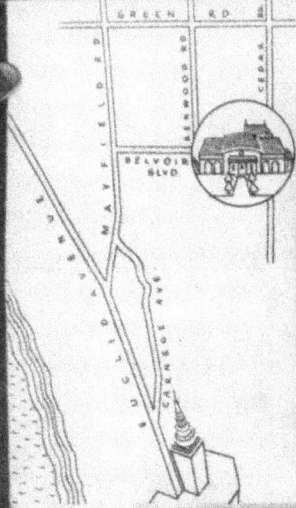

ARDELL QUINN announces the opening, on Thursday night, April 14, of a delightful suburban retreat — twenty minutes from the heart of Cleveland. Here, in a quiet setting of pastoral loveliness, one may indulge the palate with subtly prepared foods of exotic goodness. Chicken — wreathed in the aura of Maryland; steaks of buttery tenderness. There is something of the country club here . . . yet there is a charming lack of inhibiting formalities. Refreshments are reminiscent of a happier, more care-free age. Dining halls are available for larger parties, but there are also sylvan bowers for romantic tete-a-tete.

There are — but come and see for yourself. The map on this page indicates the route to follow. Come, or phone your reservation, Fairmount 4857.

HOLLYWOOD ROYAL CLUB. South Euclid's politicians were originally delighted when a supper club took up residence in the city; however, it soon became less desirable. In addition to just dinner, it offered—as the crest illustrates—wine, women, and song. (KZ.)

**SUPPER CLUB AND MORE.**
Perched just east of Belvoir
Boulevard, the club's several
entrances and exits also made
for an ideal hideout. The owner
used the club to sequester Alvin
"Creepy" Karpis, then Public
Enemy No. 1, according to the
FBI. While the club's illegal
activities had been tolerated
to that point, partly due to
many high-profile customers,
this crossed the line. (KZ.)

**CALL ME "MADAM."** Eliot Ness
of *The Untouchables* fame was
the current Cleveland safety
director. He raided the club and
arrested the owner, Ardell Quinn
(pictured). She was convicted in
1937 of violating the Mann Act
(transporting minors across state
lines for immoral purposes). (KZ.)

AMERICAN LEGION HALL POST 308

**AMERICAN LEGION HALL.** Constructed on Rushton Road in 1931 as the post office (which moved there from Mayfield and Green Roads), this building became the American Legion when the post office moved to larger quarters on Mayfield Road at Winston Road in 1938.

SOUTH EUCLID POST OFFICE 1948

**POST OFFICE.** In 1941, this post office building was erected at the corner of Winston and Mayfield Roads and served the community for many years until the current post office, named in honor of Mayor D'Amico, was built on Green Road.

# Six

# CITY SERVICES

In 1885, the city acquired a plot of land from Hannah Wade, Robert's widow, but did nothing with it until 1898 when a town hall was authorized (at a cost not to exceed $1,500). Prior to that, town meetings were held in the Old Stone School. In 1917, South Euclid incorporated as a village. By 1920, there was a connection to Cleveland city water and street lighting on Mayfield. In 1927, the city set up its first traffic light at Mayfield and Green Roads. Gas mains came in 1928.

The village was hit harder than some by the Great Depression, since many residents worked construction, which virtually stopped. Still, the village kept growing and, in 1941, achieved city status, which was marked by a five-day celebration. World War II began, and the city responded patriotically with war bond sales, blood drives, civil defense initiatives, and recycling. In 1949, a memorial honoring the 23 South Euclid sons lost to that war was dedicated.

In 1954, a more modern, larger town hall was built behind the original at a cost of $500,000. South Euclid Municipal Court had been established two years earlier. Jack Bilkey, confectionery owner and the city's first constable, had the dubious honor of arresting John D. Rockefeller and his chauffeur for speeding in 1916. By 1932, there were four policemen. In 1922, the city established a volunteer fire department. In 1923, a real siren was in place at city hall, replacing St. John Lutheran Church's bells and the Prasse Basket Factory steam whistle as the fire alarm.

**ORIGINAL CITY HALL.** This was the best city hall that the $1,500 allotted for its 1899 construction could buy. Prior to this, town meetings occurred in the Old Stone School, which was located a bit south on Green Road

South Euclid Fire Dept. 1922, Front L to r Wm. Fibich. Walter Eckert, Marshal J. H. Bilkey, Fire Chief Walter Brown, 2nd row 1 to r Mayor Charles Havre, Fred Fark, Jojn Arndt, M. Opper at wheel, Godfrey hoffmeyer, Charles Lasch, Ed Prasse, Back row 1 to r Ernst Warnke Councilman H. G. Stalnaker, Councilman Wm. Dougherty, Councilman Wm. Nolf, Court Telling Herbert Hoffmeyer and J. A. Falkner

**VOLUNTEER FIRE DEPARTMENT.** Unfortunately, the city hall had no space to park the fire engine, so a remodeling and expansion was needed.

**ADMINISTRATION, OCTOBER 1922.** Pictured, from left to right, are (first row) treasurer Walter Eckert, Councilman Charles W. Davis, Marshal Jack Bilkey, Mayor Charles Havre, and clerk Paul Prasse; (second row) Councilmen Oliver H. Whigham and O. H. Stahlnaker, William Nolf, William Dougherty, and Dan Fierbaugh.

CITY HALL, 1940s. The city hall was eventually remodeled to house the fire equipment.

South Euclid Fire Engine #3, 1945-49
In cab Carl Hauschild: on back platform L to R Howard Arndt, Wm. Fibich, Jr.
(later Chief) Gary Gold, Leo Larson   Standing Eric Pickersgill, Mayor
Lloyd N. (Bud) Reynolds, Chief Godfrey Hoffmeyer, Wm. Fibich, Sr. John
Urban, Earl Hinske, Wm. Burkheimer and Walter Graber, Squatting John Lisy
Jack Paul, A. st. Chief Joe Hodgson and Ross Al baugh

FIRE DEPARTMENT. The fire department received an upgrade as well. While still mostly volunteer, it also had three regular employees. The white Dodge fire truck was involved in a collision with a police car at Mayfield Road and Belvoir Boulevard during a blinding snowstorm. When repairs were completed, it was painted red.

CITY HALL CORNERSTONE. Here, Mayor George Urban lays the cornerstone for the new city hall building.

CORNER STONE SOUTH EUCLID CITY HALL
GEORGE URBAN MAYOR

OLD TOWN HALL          NEW CITY HALL

NEW HALL. By 1955, the new hall was complete, but the city kept the old hall in front. In 1949, South Euclid had purchased land at Monticello and Green Roads for a service facility with a major incinerator. Quite often, it spewed flaming paper from the chimney, starting small fires nearby. The city firemen would arrive with backpack-sprayers to extinguish them.

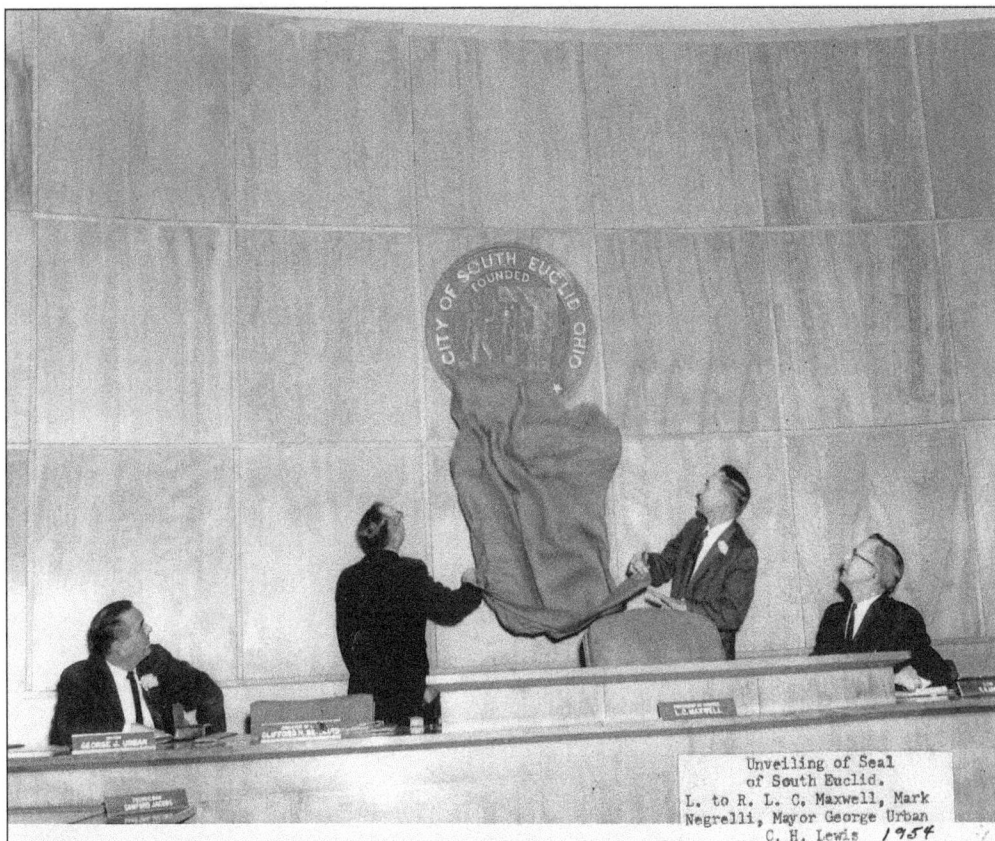

Unveiling of Seal
of South Euclid.
L. to R. L. C. Maxwell, Mark
Negrelli, Mayor George Urban
C. H. Lewis 1954

CITY SEAL. In 1959, the city accepted and adopted a city seal, designed by then finance director Lester Askue. It shows the incorporation date, 1917, and a surveyor (reminiscent of General Cleaveland's crew) next to a plat map of the city itself.

AND A FLAG. Rachel Kozan Misch, left, designed a city flag that South Euclid adopted in 1991. It shows the city seal inside a big star. That star, along with the 16 others on the border, represent Ohio as the 17th state. Ohio is also the only state without a rectangular flag. Its flag is a burgee, with a swallow-tailed end. The man holding the flag is Mayor Arnold C. D'Amico.

TRASH COLLECTION. These men pose by the carefully loaded service department truck in 1938. They are Earl Burt (left), Kenneth Ried (center), and Harvey Hansen.

GREEN ROAD DUMP. This is a filled-in quarry at the northwest corner of Green Road and Monticello Boulevard. Prior to this, it was a popular fishing hole—for those who could find the opening in the surrounding fence. Currently, trash has to be taken all the way out of Cuyahoga County.

**Streetlight.** The men in this photograph are, from left to right, Anthony Carlone, Mayor George Urban, and Gordon Artress. In this 1958 photograph, they may be discussing the much-higher efficiency of the mercury-vapor streetlamp versus incandescent lamps. South Euclid is very close to the General Electric Company's Lamp Division in East Cleveland and often an early adopter of new technologies. City streetlamps are now high-pressure sodium, and the City of South Euclid recently received a grant for LED lighting to be placed on Mayfield Road. (SUN.)

**LAW.** Judge Lawrence J. McGurk was the first judge of South Euclid Municipal Court and served from 1951 to 1960. He had previously been the city solicitor (now known as law director). His wife, Dottie, was the deputy registrar of motor vehicles.

**AND ORDER.** This is the South Euclid Police Department on May 11, 1941. Pictured are, from left to right, (seated) Capt. Fred Spence, unidentified, Martin Schmires, and Alvin Burgeson; (standing) unidentified, Bruce Burkheimer, Tony Valentino, Fred Nimberger, Pete Leonard, and unidentified. (SUN.)

# Seven

# THE NEW MILLENNIUM

Many South Euclid citizens have made it to some pretty high places, but Carl Walz topped them all. As an astronaut, he spent over six months on the International Space Station in orbit around Earth.

The new millennium brought new challenges with it. The recession and housing crisis hit Ohio in general and South Euclid in particular. In order to cut down expenses, the city furloughs nonessential employees for one day a month without pay. The city is also addressing some foreclosures through a grant for a Green initiative, rehabilitating some housing for low utility costs and first-floor living for aging. The north side of the outdated Cedar Center Shopping Center was demolished and is just now starting to be rebuilt. The Oakwood Golf Course property, partly within South Euclid, has been sold, and its use is currently indeterminate; however, some retail, senior service, and green space uses are in discussion.

While dropping enrollment forced Regina High School to close, its next-door neighbor, Notre Dame College, has been experiencing over 10 percent per year growth, prompting South Euclid to now refer to itself as "A College Town for All Ages."

**ASTRONAUT CARL WALZ.** Carl Walz grew up in South Euclid and attended Brush High School, then went on to Ohio's Kent State University. He returned to nearby John Carroll University and obtained his master's degree in solid state physics. Walz joined NASA and has served on shuttle flights aboard the *Discovery, Columbia, Atlantis,* and *Endeavour.* (NASA.)

**SpaceWalz.** On a 1993 space walk, Walz waves at his colleagues from the aft end of *Discovery's* payload bay. He is evaluating tools, tethers, and a foot restraint. (NASA.)

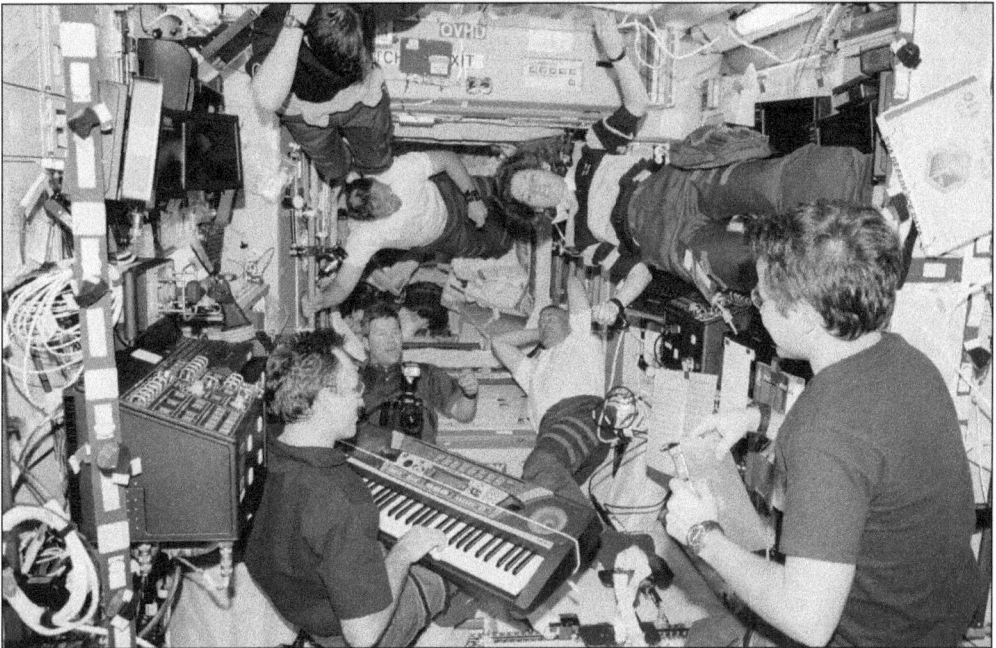

**Space Jam.** Carl Walz spent over six months on the International Space Station from 2001 to 2002. He asked for a keyboard as one of his few personal items allowed. The many months on the station afford some discretionary time. "Get down" does not mean anything in a weightless environment. (NASA.)

CEDAR CENTER. Cedar Center North was demolished in 2009, anticipating a rebuilding and modernization of this shopping center. The recession slowed progress, but in late 2010, the city came to an agreement with Gordon Food Service to build an anchor store at the site. This was the ground-breaking ceremony.

GORDON FOOD SERVICE. Construction is well underway on the new food store, the first of many planned businesses in the revitalized Cedar Center North.

**CONCRETE.** Decades ago, lining creeks seemed like a good idea. This was the result on an exposed section of Nine Mile Creek. (JG.)

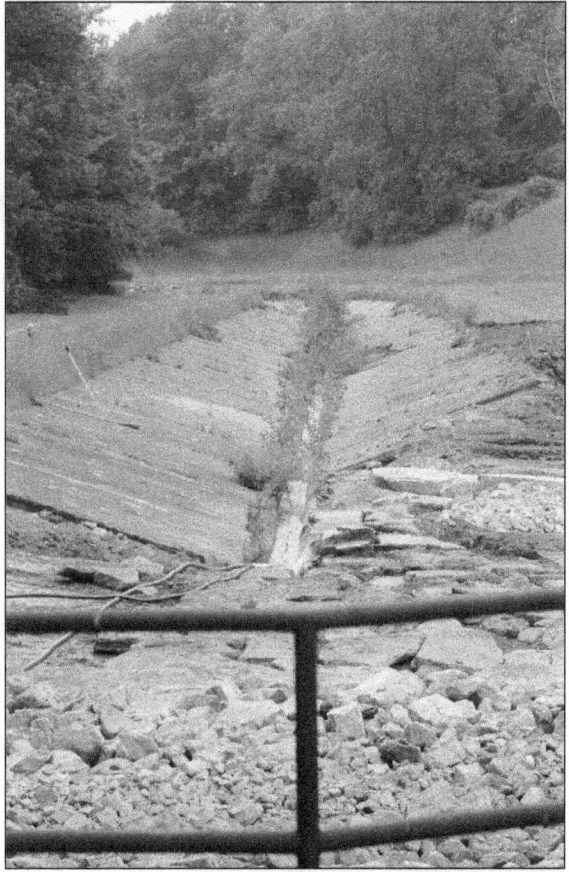

**TO WETLAND.** The stream was restored to its natural wetland state, much to the delight of local conservationists as well as denizens of the local environment. (JG.)

**MEMORIAL DAY PARADE.** Monday, May 30, 2011 was a bright, warm, welcoming morning for South Euclid's annual Memorial Day parade. Here, early in the parade, the bagpipers are playing "Scotland the Brave" and other traditional tunes.

**MARCHING BAND.** The Brush High School Marching Band turned out in force. The parade route starts on Green Road north of Cedar Road and proceeds along Green Road to the memorial site at Anderson Road.

**ROCKET CAR.** The rocket ships were a popular ride at the long-defunct Euclid Beach Amusement Park. Ron Heitman, who was an owner of Washington-Lee Service in Cleveland Heights, purchased this one and made it street-ready. The car participates in many local parades and events and, in this image, is piloted by Ron's daughter.

**MAYOR.** The current mayor, Georgine Welo, rides with her husband, Carter, in the parade. Carter is an owner of South Euclid Hardware. In 2011, a decision was made that not only officeholders, but also those running for office, could participate in the parade together with political signs. Many such displays were present.

**OAKWOOD.** Oakwood Country Club was founded in 1905 by several of the city's prominent Jewish business and civic leaders. Its declining membership caused it to close, and Oakwood merged with Mayfield Country Club.

**OAKWOOD TOMORROW.** Although the details and requisite zoning changes have yet to be worked out, the purchaser, First Interstate Properties of Lyndhurst, is planning some housing, retail, and green space.

**PLAYGROUND OF POSSIBILITIES.** In the fall of 2009, over 1,500 residents and businesses contributed to the building of the Playground of Possibilities in Bexley Park. The playground opened in the spring of 2010.

**A PLACE FOR SWINGERS.** This place for swinging, crawling, and climbing was particularly friendly to wheelchair access and children with other disabilities and challenges.

**TUNNELS AND MORE.** It featured tunnels, slides, a bridge, a rocker panel, and all sorts of other nooks and crannies to explore.

**OPEN AREA.** The playground also had open area covered with shredded rubber that, while easy on feet, was hard on wheelchairs and proved to be all too flammable.

**FIRE!** The playground was constructed from recycled materials, including this shredded-rubber ground cover. While this material was not easy to light on fire, the flare found by three teenagers a few days after Halloween 2010 did the trick. The blaze was very hard to stop and destroyed the entire playground. Promising to rebuild, hundreds of residents attended a rally a few days later under near-blizzard conditions.

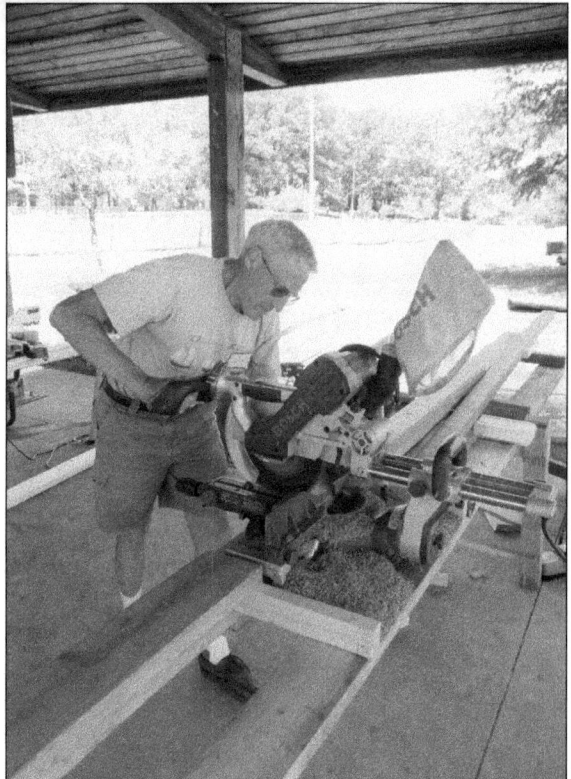

**REBUILDING.** Volunteer Jay Freer is sawing one of the hundreds of beams of Trex for the rebuilt playground. This pseudolumber is made from sawdust and other discarded wood parts molded together with a multitude of recycled plastic grocery bags. Freer is also active on the South Euclid Recycling Committee. The ground is now covered with a less-flammable rubber mat. In 2011, the entire playground was rebuilt between June and August.

# BIBLIOGRAPHY

Horwitz, Samuel J., Carl F. Doershuk, and Nancy C. Erdey, eds. *For the Children: 120 Years of Rainbow Babies & Children's Hospital.* Cleveland, OH: University Hospitals Health System, 2007.

Keyerleber, Karl and the Lyndhurst Historical Committee. *Hometown: The Story of Lyndhurst.* Lyndhurst, OH, 1950.

Larick, Roy and Craig Semsel. *Euclid Township, 1796–1801: Protest in the Western Reserve.* Cleveland,OH: Western Reserve Historical Society, 2003.

Palermo, Anthony. *Our Own Little Red Schoolhouse.* South Euclid, OH: South Euclid Historical Society, 1976.

Schuemann, Nancy L. *On the Threshold of a New Century: The City of South Euclid, 1967–1999.* Cleveland, OH: August Graphics Inc., 1999.

South Euclid Golden Jubilee Book Committee. *The Proud Heritage of South Euclid, Ohio (Golden Jubilee 1917–1967, South Euclid).* South Euclid, OH: Golden Jubilee Book Committee, 1967

# ABOUT THE HISTORICAL SOCIETY

In 1966, a small group of citizens, led in no small part by Mayor George Urban and his wife, Helen, decided that the time had come to preserve the legacy of South Euclid. Thus, the South Euclid Historical Society was officially established. This small portion of the Western Reserve had its importance, especially with its farms, Euclid bluestone, sandstone quarries, and basket factories.

Many of the residents had accumulated items of interest to others, and these were offered to the society. With no place to put them, the society began the search for a location to call home. The South Euclid-Lyndhurst Branch of the Cuyahoga County Public Library System was, and still is, located in the former mansion of entrepreneur William E. Telling. An offer was made by library officers in 1977 to allow the society to locate in the five-room quarters previously occupied by the caretaker. The resulting museum now has an outstanding collection of artifacts that includes items from the 1800s to the present. In 2009, the society voted to include the neighboring community of Lyndhurst in its scope, as that city no longer had an active historical society.

As an outreach, children from all of the South Euclid-Lyndhurst City elementary schools make a yearly visit to the museum, and the society holds regular meetings that are open to all. New members are welcome at a very nominal fee. Its website can be accessed at either SouthEuclidHistory.org or LyndhurstHistory.org and e-mail addressed to either info@southeuclidhistory.org or info@lyndhursthistory.org.

Please join us as we approach South Euclid's 100th anniversary (in 2017) of becoming a village. The South Euclid-Lyndhurst Historical Society is a nonprofit organization with IRS 501(c)3 tax-exempt status.

Visit us at
arcadiapublishing.com

www.ingramcontent.com/pod-product-compliance
Lightning Source LLC
Chambersburg PA
CBHW050555110426
42813CB00008B/2368

* 9 7 8 1 5 3 1 6 5 4 9 1 7 *